POLLEN AS EVIDENCE

VOLUME 2, ISSUE 4 OF BRILLOPEDIA

GARIMA OBEROI

Contents

Preface

"Start writing, no matter what. The water does not flow until the faucet is turned on".

- Louis L'Amour

Hundreds of students and professors are contributing their work to Brillopedia, we are here to provide ample information about Law and Contemporary issues. Our aim is to provide a platform for today's generation to express their views and ideas on law and contemporary law.

Author

CHAPTER ONE

ABSTRACT

Forensic palynology, the use of pollen and spores to assist in solving criminal and civil cases, is a highly underutilized and neglected technique. During the past century, there have been only limited attempts to use pollen and spore evidence in either criminal or civil cases for a variety of reasons, including a lack of available information about the technique, a very limited number of specialists trained to do this type of forensic work, and an almost total absence of academic centers that are capable of training needed pollen specialists or forensic facilities able, or willing, to fund research in this area. Pollen from spermatophytes, fungi, ferns and bryophytes as well as other organic-walled microfossils likedin of lagellates and a critarches, are all included under the umbrella term palynomorph. The area of forensic botany has been significantly impacted by developments in plant genetics. Pollen DNA profiling has yet to be used in forensic investigations, nevertheless.

Pollen was once used as a sort of botanical dust debris in several forensic examinations that used dust traces. Comparative morphological information, hints to unanticipated elements of breeding systems, pollination biology, and hybridization can all be found in the study of pollen grains.[1]Palynological evidence can offer incredibly strong associative and investigative evidence. Never the less, the effectiveness of palynology in forensic research has been uneven. There are numerous anecdotal instances when pollen evidence has achieved outstanding results.

But because it is labor-intensive, takes a great deal of knowledge and experience, lacks over sight over sample collection, lacks proper resources and funding, and is not widely renowned for its ability to solve crimes, it is grossly underutilized in most countries. Palynology has been applied to forensic issues in an unorganized manner, leaving the basic ideas without systematic debate. There is a need to establish palynological evidence through validation-type investigations and experiments, the introduction of independent proficiency testing, and the reevaluation of the acceptability of most evidence forms in the current legal climate.[2]

Keywords- Pollen, Evidence, Palynology, Forensic, Investigation

CHAPTER TWO

INTRODUCTION

When it comes to legal evidence, forensic palynology generally focuses on the analysis of pollen and spores connected to crime scenes and other legal-related contexts. Even though it has been practiced as a discipline for a little over 50 years, it is still mostly unheard of in many parts of the world. Despite its promise, for ensicpalynology is only occasionally regarded as a helpful approach, except for a few nations like the United Kingdom and NewZealand.[1]

The underutilization of this approach across the globe is thought to be caused by a variety of factors. First, there is the issue of general acceptance by legal systems and law enforcement organizations, which is primarily related to the reliability of pollen data being questioned and a lack of awareness of specific case applications that might be helped by looking at the associatedpollen or spore evidence. The absence of qualified scientists in the field of forensic paleontologyis a second contributing issue. One needs expertise in the study of pollen and spores as well as a thorough understanding of plantecology, botany, and taxonomy to be competent in this field.

One of the issues relates to the validity of employing pollen and spore data as forensic evidence, as perceived by the legal system and law enforcement officials. The physical distinctions between each species of plant are frequently extremely minute since each plant species produces a distinct spore typer pollen article. Most forensic pollen and spore investigations rely on light microscopy for examination, however at this level, the accuracy required for species identification is frequently not achievable. With the additional resolution obtained by using a scanning electron microscope (SEM), this level of added precision can frequently be resolved for individual pollen types and even for conducting total pollen analyses of a sample; however, the cost in terms of time and funding typically makes this alternative inappropriate for the majority of forensic use.

Forensic palynologists relyon documenting the ratios of each pollen type as well as the total pollen and spore makeup of a sample. A high level of analysis precision is provided by this combination. Typically, forensic pollen experts present their findings in probabilistic terms and then support them with examples from their experience. There is a high likelihood that a match will result from the combination of pollen identifications (often down to the genus level), along with quantitative ratios of each pollen and spore taxon. Finally, due to the nature of forensic pollen and spore data and the nearly infinite number of potential variables that must be taken into account, most statistical techniques, such the likelihood ratio, cannot be applied effectively. When relying on forensic pollen and spore data, one should be more concerned with the expertise, ability, and research experience of the pollen analysis.[2]

CHAPTER THREE

TYPES OF POLLEN

Some of the most useful types of pollen and spores for forensics are the wind-pollinated types. This group includes the spore-producing plants such as ferns and mosses, the fungi, and a wide range of pollen types produced by the gymnosperms (non flowering seed-bearing plants such as pines, cedars, and spruce), and a significant number of angiosperms (flowering seed-bearing plants such as aspen, elms, and oaks). Because wind pollination is a less reliable method of dispersion, these plants must produce vast quantities of pollen or spores that are usually light weight and area erodynamically designed to travel easily in air currents. The enormity of pollen production in many of the wind-pollinated (anemophilous) plants is exemplified by statistics such as follows: a single branch of a marijuana (Cannabis) plant can produce about 500 million pollen grains, one her baceousdock (Rumex) plant produces a total of about 400 million pollen grains, a single panicle of sorghum grass (Sorghum) disperses about 100 million pollen grains, and just one malestrobiluson a branch of a lodge polepine (Pinus contorta) produces over 600,000 pollen grains. Some of the most useful types of pollen and spores for forensics are the wind-pollinated types. This group includes the spore-producing plants such as ferns and mosses, the fungi, and a wide range of pollen types produced by the gymnosperms (non-flowering seed-bearing plants such as pines, cedars and spruce), and a significant number of angiosperms (flowering seed-bearing plants such as aspen, elms and oaks). Because wind pollination is a less reliable method of dispersion, these plants must produce vast quantities of pollen or spores that are usually light weight and are aerodynamically designed to travel easily in air currents. The enormity of pollen production in many of the wind-pollinated (anemophilous) plants is exemplified by statistics such as follows: a single branch of amarijuana (Cannabis) plant can produce about 500 million pollen grains, one herbaceous dock(Rumex) plant produces a total of about 400 million pollen grains, a single panicle of sorghumgrass (Sorghum) disperses about100 million pollen grains and just on emalestrobilus on a branch of a lodge polepine (Pinuscontorta) produces over 600,000 pollen grains. Some of the most useful types of pollen and spores for forensics are the wind-pollinated types. This group includes the spore-producing plants such as ferns and mosses, the fungi, and a wide range of pollen types produced by the gymnosperms (non flowering seed-bearing plants such as pines, cedars, and spruce), and a significant number of angiosperms (flowering seed-bearing plants such as aspen, elms and oaks). Because wind pollination is a less reliable method of dispersion, these plants must produce vast quantities of pollen or spores that are usually lightweight and are aerodynamically designed to travel easily in air currents. The enormity of pollen production in many of the wind-pollinated (anemophilous) plants is exemplified by statistics such as follows: a single branch of amarijuana (Cannabis) plant can produce about 500 million pollen grains, one herbaceous dock (Rumex) plant produces a total of about 400 million pollen grains, a single panicle of sorghumgrass (Sorghum) dispersesabout 100 million pollen grains, and just on emalestrobilusona branch of a lodgepole pine (Pinus contorta) produces over 600,000 pollen grains.

The wind-pollinated varieties of pollen and spores are some of the most helpful kinds for forensics. This group comprises fungi, spore-producing plants like ferns and mosses, a variety of pollen Generated by gymnosperms (non flowering seed-bearing plants like pines, cedars, and spruce), as well as a sizeable number of angiosperms (flowering seed-bearing plants like aspen, elms, and oaks).These plants must generate enormous amounts of pollen or spores, which are typically light and aerodynamically built to flow well in air currents because wind pollination is a less reliable mode of dissemination.

The enormity of pollen production in many of the wind-pollinated (anemophilous) plants is exemplified by statistics such as follows: a single branch of a marijuana (Cannabis) plant can produce about 500 million pollen grains, one herbaceous dock (Rumex) plant produces a total of about 400 million pollen grains, a single panicle of sorghum grass (Sorghum) disperses about 100 million pollen grains, and just one male strobilus on a branch of a lodge pole pine (Pinuscontorta) produces over 600,000 pollen grains Numerous wind-pollinated (anemophilous) plants produce enormous amounts of pollen, as shown by the following statistics: About 500 million pollen grains can be produced by a single branch of a marijuana plant (Cannabis), 400 million by a single her baceousdock plant (Rumex), 100 million by a single panicle of sorghumgrass (Sorghum), andover 600,000 by a single male strobiluson a branch of a lodge polepine (Pinus contorta).

Many more wind-pollinated plants, including ragweed, grasses, some kinds of eucalyptus, filberts, hickory, walnut, birch, alder, and elms, generate between 10,000 and 100,000 pollen grains peranther in addition to these examples (the part of a flower that produces and contains pollen and is usually borne on a stalk).

CHAPTER FOUR

POLLEN AS A FORENSIC TOOL

There are four crucial factors that underpin the reasons why pollen and spores are useful forensic instruments:-

The great majority of these palynomorphs are first released into the air by a variety of plants that produce pollen and spores. Air currents then carry these palynomorphs and finally cause them to fall to the ground as a thin covering known as pollen rain (total pollen deposited annually at any given location). In some areas, the volume of pollen and spores disseminated is so high that the pollen rain causes exposed land and water surfaces to be come yellow. The pollen rain in every location of the world provides a snapshot of that area's vegetation and creates a "pollen print" that can be used to help identify the region, even though it is not an accurate measurement of the surrounding vegetation and consequently the area's climate.[1]

Second, pollen and spores can become caught on nearly any kind of surface because they are small, visually invisible particles. It follows that at any location, pollen or spores from local plants, or more precisely, pollen and spores from a particular crime scene, can serve as evidence to connect a suspect or an item to the area or crime scene.[2]

Third, there are around 500,000 distinct plant species that either generate pollen or spores. Thankfully, each of these species produces pollen or spores that can be recognized as being from the parent plant. However, frequently, variations in the pollen and spores of closely related species or even related genera may appear so similar that precise identification can only be achieved through in-depth studies using the high-resolution capabilities of a SEM or a transmission electron microscope (TEM), or both. However, using these microscopy techniques becomes difficult due to the time and cost involved, as well as the general absence of extensive pollen and spore reference materials for comparisons. Therefore, for the majority of problems, requiring accurate matches of a pollen type to an exact species level of identification becomes impracticable or too expensive, especially in genera with hundreds of species, like Clematis, which has over 220 recognized species.[3]

Fourth, the majority of pollen and spores are quite resilient to deterioration. So, pollen and spore evidence from a place or a crime scene might last for years, hundreds of years, even thousands and millions of years. The trapped pollen and spores can still be recovered and utilized as evidence to aid investigators if crime scene evidence is handled and maintained properly years or decades afterwards. There are certain exceptions, including in fields that have been ploughed or places where so ilis frequently wet and dried, where pollen and spores disintegrate very quickly.[4]

CHAPTER FIVE

FORENSIC PALYNOLOGY

Over 50 years ago, forensic psychology became a tool for law enforcement. The use of pollen and spores in forensic palynology is used to resolve legal disputes, whether they are civil or criminal. You can collect pollen and spores from are mark ably diverse spectrum of things, including human beings. Indicators of the origin of the goods and the features of the ecosystems from which the material on them is sourced include pollen and spores. Their abundance, dispersal methods, resistance to mechanical and chemical break down, tiny size, and for mare all factors that contribute to their value. Their frequently intricate form enables identification to a single parent plant tax on that can be linked to a particular biological region or scenario.[1]

Pollen and spore assemblages, which can easily remove from areas of interest without giving a suspect any visual cues as to what has happened, characterize many settings and scenarios. The future of this area of forensic science is secured thanks to the numerous publications and high-profile cases involving forensic palynology and environmental analysis that have recently gained attention. Additionally, law enforcement organizations now have access to far more in-depth data thanks to the development of multidisciplinary approaches to environmental investigations of crime scenes, enabling them to more precisely predict what might have occurred during the commission of criminal activities.[2]

CHAPTER SIX

POLLEN A STRACE EVIDENCE INFORENSICS

A younger girl, about 15 years old, was murdered on November 10, 1979, and her body was dumped in a cornfield just outside the sleepy town of Caledonia, New York. She did not match any records of missing people, and she lacke didientification. She was buried in an ear by cemetery with a headstone bearing the inscription "Jane Doe," becoming yet another "cold case." The body was unearthed, and DNA examined in 2005 in the hopes that it would reveal an ID, but even that failed to produce any fresh leads. In 2006, John York, the first copto look into the murderin1979, decided to attempt a novel method he had read about on the internet called "forensic pollen analysis."

I was contacted and sent the girl's garments, which were still in the original evidence bags sealed and kept by them edical examiner more than 25years previously, as I was the only scientist at the time who performed this type of examination. Every piece of her original clothes, including the lint in the bottom of her pockets, was carefully vacuumed, and the results showed a variety of pollen kinds, many of which might be linked to the plants present in the cornfield where she was slain. However, she found a few pollen grains in the bottom of her pockets from tropical plants that are only found in Southern Florida and Southern California and don't grow in New York.

That implied that, prior to her death, she must have resided in or recently been to either Florida or California. A second search was conducted with a southern focus based on the pollen information. She was eventually recognized as Tammy to Alexander, a 16-year-old who fled her family in 1979, in 2015. She was from southern Florida, exactly as the pollen had predicted.

Forensic palynology (pollen studies) has historically concentrated on obtaining legal evidence through the examination of pollen and spores connected to crime scenes and other legal-related circumstances. Although it has been practiced as a discipline for a little over 50 years, it is still mostly unheard of in many parts of the world.

CHAPTER SEVEN

ROLE OF POLLEN IN INDIAN SCENARIO

The team compared the data with the current pollen forms of Crotonoideae and looked for any parallels with previously recorded fossils on a world wide scale. The team investigated pollen fossil samples from sediments obtained at four locations in Madhya Pradesh, Rajasthan, and Gujarat. Alight microscope and a scanning electron microscope were also used to examine the pollen that had been collected.[1]

Following a thorough morphological analysis, they concluded that the pollen fossil discovered in India resembled living members of the Crotonoideae family including the plants Jatropha, Croton, Endospermum, Klaineanthus, Blachia, and Tetrochidium. Currently, tropical rain forests in Southeast Asia and Africa are home to Endo spermum and Klaine an thus pollen plants, respectively. However, the current study discovered their pollen in Indian sediments that are 66–54 million years old. The pollen of the plant Blachia was discovered in the current study as the first-ever fossil evidence from Gujarat mines.

A species of the plant Tetrorchidium, which is currently indigenous to South America, was also discovered in sediments from Central India that are 68–66 million years old. The sediments date back to a time when India and Africa were intertwined. Tetrorchidium originated in Africa, according to the study, and was later spread to South America and India when the threel and masses were still relatively close to one another.

The discovery of Blachia pollen fossils in the current study is a prime illustration of how the collision of the Indian and Asian plates encouraged evolution. However, one of the Blachia species, which had previously been found throughout the Indian subcontinent, later withdrew to isolated pockets in the moist Myristica swamps of the southern Western Ghats.

Biogeographic studies benefit from pollen fossil exploration and recovery because they fill in the gaps in the pollen fossil records that currently exist from different geographic regions. The data can be used to create a paleo biogeographic history of the important Croto noideae plant family.

The primitive group (ancestral group) of the Euphorbiaceae family of flowering plants, which includes the Croton type pollen, is called Croto no ideae. Pollen features such pollen wall thickness, shape, and apices changed dramatically over time as the Croton type pollen changed in response to shifting climatic circumstances. This work widens the potential applications of phylogenetic analysis (study based on physical properties and genetic factors). The analysis would further aid in identifying the species within the genus Euphorbiaceae that are closely related and those that have evolved and separated due to new physical and climatic barriers.

The environment on the Indian plate under went a significant change during the journey a sit drifted from Pange a in the south and collided with the Asian plate in the north. A few kinds of pollen adjusted the introits to adapt to the new climate, but many pollen did not with stand the new climatic circumstances while travelling. Following the India-Asia collision, the Himalayan mountains' elevation and the subsequent occurrence of seasonal aridity limited the further distribution of moist pollen from India to Southeast Asia. As a result, several Crotonoideae species, including the Blachia species, became unique to India or became endemic to that country.

CHAPTER EIGHT

CONCLUSION

Despite the fact that forensic pollen studies are still being used and applied in many parts of the world, there is mounting evidence that they have value as forensic evidence. The demand for trained professionals in this field will rise as more and more law enforcement agencies realise the potential utility of forensic pollen work, which will put more focus on encouraging the construction of training facilities for these specialists. Pollen and spore studies are valuable forensic tools, and several nations (including the United Kingdom and New Zealand) and some law enforcement organizations in other nations are already aware of this.

Pollen evidence is infrequently gathered at crime scenes in other nations, and there doesn't seem to be much contemporary interest in exploiting pollen and spores for their possible forensic applications. Noting some of the significant ways in which pollen evidence has already proven effective in giving evidence that helped solve criminal and civil cases may be one method to raise attention to an under utilised forensic technique. Homicide, terrorism, genocide, bombings, forgery, robbery, rape, arson, counterfeiting, production and sale of illegal substances, assault, hit-and-run incidents, poaching, and identity theft are just a few of the crimes for which pollen and spore evidence has been used.